British and European
Trucks
of the 1970s

Those were the days ...™

SPIERS of MELKSHAM

A E C MANDATOR

TGU 205M

BERTOMEU

VELOCE

Also from Veloce –

www.veloce.co.uk

First published in November 2012 by Veloce Publishing Limited, Veloce House, Parkway Farm Business Park, Middle Farm Way, Poundbury, Dorchester, Dorset, DT1 3AR, England.
Fax 01305 250479/e-mail info@veloce.co.uk/web www.veloce.co.uk or www.velocebooks.com.

ISBN: 978-1-845844-15-8 UPC: 6-36847-04415-2

Readers with ideas for automotive books, or books on other transport or related hobby subjects, are invited to write to the editorial director of Veloce Publishing at the above address.
British Library Cataloguing in Publication Data – A catalogue record for this book is available from the British Library.
Typesetting, design and page make-up all by Veloce Publishing Ltd on Apple Mac. Printed in India by Replika Press.

Contents

Foreword & Acknowledgements

Foreword

As the swinging sixties swung into the 1970s there was an impending air of change hanging over the European trucking industry. Britain had not yet joined the European Economic Community (EEC), as it was to become known, and so its trucks and trucking legislation had developed in complete isolation from mainland Europe.

The 1970s typified everything that was both right and wrong with the British trucking industry. At the start of the decade full order books and long delivery times on new vehicles resulted in reluctance by British manufacturers to invest in improving the specification of maximum weight trucks. This allowed European manufacturers to make steady in-roads into UK fleets, and, by the end of the 1970s, such well-respected names as AEC, Albion, Atkinson, BMC, Commer, Guy, and Thornycroft had all been consigned to the history books.

From a driver's perspective, roping and sheeting to secure loads was still an everyday requirement, and ISO containers and newfangled curtain side trailers were yet to become mainstream. The British government set the required minimum of 6bhp per ton for operation at 32 tons gross vehicle weight (GVW), and the basic UK motorway network was still under construction.

Against this background, the prospect of changes to gross vehicle weights was high on the agenda of most operators, and with Germany already allowing operation at 38 tons GVW, there was speculation that UK weight limits could be increased to 34, 38 or even 44 tons once Britain finally joined the EEC.

Despite the slow decline in UK sales of home-produced vehicles, confident British Leyland chairman Lord Stokes commented in 1974 that much of this lost business was a backlog which British industry would have to supply at some stage, and added that there was inevitability about business coming back. During 1973 BLMC had increased its market penetration to 31 per cent in the UK, and the corporation's export sales remained at 48 per cent of production.

However, perhaps he should have heeded the words of Kenneth Cook, the then managing director of Midlands BRS who, in the same week, announced that British Road Services was being compelled to buy foreign trucks because British manufacturers were unable to meet demand. The BRS Midlands fleet of more than 1100 vehicles, which had been 100 per cent British at the beginning of 1973, had vehicles of foreign manufacture making up 25 per cent of its fleet 12 months later.

Who could have predicted, at the start of the decade, that the flood of European manufacturers into Britain – no doubt riding on the back of the runaway success of Volvo and Scania – would rapidly reach a point where at one stage no fewer than 20 different makes of maximum gross weight vehicles were available to operators.

In addition, many of Britain's manufacturers of medium weight trucks saw their niche market diminishing as many operators upsized to maximum gross weight vehicles by acquiring cheap foreign imports. So, whilst manufacturers of traditional heavyweights looked towards 35-38 tonnes and beyond, manufacturers at the lighter end of the market flooded the market with noisy V8-powered 28 tonners pretending to be 32 tonners. It was a crowded, but colourful truck market and one which we'll never see the likes of again.

This book focuses exclusively on trucks built by manufacturers based in Britain or Europe, wherever they may have been used. However, it does not attempt to be the definitive guide to the decade, nor does it attempt to be a concise catalogue of every make and model produced. With some 63 different manufacturers to squeeze in, in some cases the reference is no more than a snapshot.

Colin Peck
Wraysbury, England

Acknowledgements

I would like to dedicate this book to the large number of people, literally from around the world, including truck manufacturers, dealers, drivers, journalists and enthusiasts, without whose help this book would not have been possible.

Many who worked in the trucking industry during the 1970s have fond memories of those days, and this book is a tribute to a decade of amazing change, and to a vast array of manufacturers the likes of which we'll never see again.

It won't be possible to mention everybody who had a part in making this book possible, but I will list as many as I can:

Big Lorry Blog (UK)
British Commercial Vehicle Museum, Leyland (BCVM)

Gyles Carpenter
Max Chern
Bill Clowes
Richard Creswell
Clive Davis
Fleet Transport (Ireland)
Les Freathy
Chris Gardner
David Gothard
Juraj Hlavac
Martin Hayes
Arthur Ingram
David Jaffrey
Niels Jansen
Trevor Jones
Ralf Koch
David Lowe
Lex Meeder
Rik Meeder
John Ormandy
Tony Pain (DAF UK)
Bill Reid
Len Rogers
Rod Simmonds
Richard Stanier
Transport News Magazine

British manufacturers

AEC

The Associated Equipment Company (AEC) proved that despite having a history dating back to 1912, a loyal customer base and a reputation as 'Builders of London's Buses,' you can still go to the wall if internal politics and bean-counters conspire against you.

So, whilst the merger of Leyland and AEC in 1962 should have been a catalyst for great things for the new company, as both truck builders had full order books and

Despite Leyland's refusal to fund development of the V8-800, AEC worked on the engine behind closed doors, and managed to extract 275bhp from a turbocharged version in 1972 before the Leyland axe fell on the project.
(Courtesy BCVM)

AEC's truck for the 1970s, the ill-fated Mandator V8, was short-lived due to lack of development.
(Courtesy BCVM)

established export markets, the relationship proved less than beneficial in the long-term for the Southall-based truck builder. In addition, the 1968 merger of Leyland and BMC, which included GUY Motors and a plethora of car and van builders, brought even more model duplication, as well as serious financial and labour problems associated with the car-making divisions.

This Belgian-cabbed AEC Mercury gives a whole new twist to the Ergomatic theme. (Courtesy BCVM)

Leyland refused AEC access to the high-datum Ergomatic cab, as used on the Leyland Buffalo, so AEC built its own, which, sadly, never got beyond the prototype stage. (Courtesy BCVM)

AEC had built the iconic Routemaster bus, which is still working selected tourist routes in London more than 50 years after it was first introduced, and had been producing trucks that were usually the most powerful in their class. It had an immensely loyal customer base, and sales even increased for a while when the new Leyland-group 'Ergomatic' truck cab was introduced across the AEC, Albion and Leyland brands for the first time in 1964.

That loyalty even remained after the debacle with the ill-fated V8-800 engine that briefly saw the light of day in 1968. Designed from the outset for eventual turbocharging and inter-cooling, with a potential output of 400bhp, the 12,154cc V8 produced 247bhp and a surprisingly low 580lb/ft of torque, which meant that it needed to be kept revving for maximum performance.

Unusual Mandator drawbar outfit.
(Courtesy BCVM)

Mammoth Major 8x4. (Courtesy Gyles Carpenter)

The concept of building an engine with which to compete against powerful European trucks, which were steadily increasing in popularity in the UK, was sound, but the project was under-funded by Leyland, and so was launched prematurely and underdeveloped. Whilst the AEC Mandator V8 took the commercial vehicle industry by storm at its introduction, it was destined to fail miserably.

Overheating, big end bearing problems, and troublesome semi-automatic gearboxes resulted in the model being withdrawn within months of its introduction, and AEC proceeded to buy back most of them. Even so, the customer base remained loyal, and, by the end of Mandator production in July 1977, the 12,473cc top-of-the-range AV760 straight-six engine had been uprated to 265bhp at 2200rpm. However, in reality, it was too little too late.

In 1971, Leyland took the decision to build the new premium heavyweight T25 truck range (eventually to be known as the Marathon) at AEC's Southall plant, which was running at 77 per cent capacity compared with

Mammoth Major 6x4. (Courtesy BCVM)

The Leyland Marathon was designed from the outset as a high specification truck capable of combating the rising number of European trucks being operated by British firms. With the demise of the ill-fated V8-800 engine, the only engine within the entire Leyland group capable of being developed further was the AEC AV760 straight six. Re-engineered as the turbocharged TL12, it produced 280bhp.

Launched in 1973, the Marathon could not, however, be regarded as a true AEC, as it wasn't directly developed from a preceding model. That didn't stop operators loyal to the AEC brand purchasing them, with some even replacing the Leyland grille badge with that of AEC.

Unfortunately, the Marathon was also a victim of Leyland's lack of investment and foresight, as it was denied the brand new cab that would have made it really successful. Instead, it got the standard Sankey (later GKN) cab, raised higher than normal, but with a 'cobbled together' look. The Marathon performed well, but drivers complained of poor fit and finish, and Cummins engines were introduced to overcome problems with the TL12 unit.

Leyland had always been the dominant force in the merger with AEC, and by degrees the design and manufacturing facilities at Southall were sidelined. With parent group, British Leyland Motor Corporation, virtually bankrupt by 1974, investment in and expansion of the AEC plant came to a halt. Production levels fell, popular models were axed in favour of less popular and troublesome new Leyland models, yet loyal customers stubbornly waited for new AECs that were becoming increasingly difficult to obtain.

On the 25th May 1979, the AEC factory at Southall closed with the loss of 2150 jobs. It was

almost 100 per cent at Leyland. However, whilst AEC also proposed to re-launch the Mandator with an improved V8, politics within the Leyland management conspired against the plan and it was consigned to history.

Launched in 1973, the Leyland Marathon was built at AEC's Southall plant. (Courtesy BCVM)

A Leyland Marathon was the last truck down the AEC line before Leyland closed the plant in 1979. (Courtesy BCVM)

a needless and premature end for one of Britain's most respected vehicle manufacturers, but against a background of bitter rivalry and the settling of old scores at boardroom level, it's thought that Lord Stokes (the then head of British Leyland) raised a toast to the demise of AEC, after all, he had been turned down as an apprentice at the Southall works many years before.

Albion

Scotland-based Albion was acquired by Leyland Motors in 1951 and, despite cut backs to its model range, quickly found its niche as the builder of light and medium-weight vehicles within the group. However, after the British Leyland Motor Corporation was formed in 1968, which then brought competing models from Guy- and Bathgate-built BMC into the group, Albion's days as a separate brand were numbered.

When the Sankey-built Ergomatic tilting cab was introduced in 1964, Albion also continued using the older Motor Panels-built Leyland-Albion-Dodge (LAD) cab, which reduced unladen weight and proved particularly popular with operators in Scotland. Both cab variants were used until 1972, when the Albion brand

The Albion Chieftain was popular with general haulage contractors across the UK. (Courtesy Dave Gothard)

The ubiquitous LAD-cabbed Albion Reiver was the workhorse of the UK construction industry. (Courtesy BCVM)

was discontinued by Leyland in favour of the parent company badge, and the company became Leyland Glasgow.

The new Scotstoun, Glasgow-built Leylands used a re-styled version of the Bathgate G series cab, itself developed from the old BMC FJ cab introduced in 1964. Production of Chieftain, Clydesdale and Reiver models continued at Scotstoun until 1980, when manufacturing was transferred to Leyland's Bathgate plant.

This shot of the British Leyland group stand at the 1971 Earls Court CV Show has a line-up of prototype Albions sporting the high-datum Ergomatic cab as fitted to the Leyland Buffalo range. Unfortunately, these never made it into production, as Leyland ditched the Albion brand a year later, rebranded the trucks as Leylands, and fitted the Bathgate G-series cab. (Courtesy BCVM)

The Ergomatic cab version of the Albion Reiver, although more modern, was never as popular as the lightweight LAD-cabbed version. (Courtesy Bill Clowes)

Argyle

1970 saw a new Scottish truck manufacturer appear, albeit too briefly. The East Kilbride-based Argyle Motor Manufacturing Company launched its 16-ton GVW two-axle rigid, known as the Argyle Christina, powered by the trusty Perkins 6.354 120bhp diesel, and fitted with a version of the Motor Panels cabs as used, at the time, by Guy and Seddon.

Whilst the truck sold well to local haulage companies, Argyle failed to compete against the might of major truck manufacturers, and production ceased a year later. Estimates vary on how many were built, but it's thought the total was less than ten.

Atkinson

The 1970s proved amazingly disastrous for British truck manufacturers with names starting with the letter A. However, unlike AEC and Albion, whose demise was purely down to internal politics within the ill-fated Leyland empire, the fate of Atkinson was not of its own making.

The Walton-le-Dale truck builder started the decade with plans to build 2000 trucks a year – with 18 months' worth of orders on its books, it was in confident mood. However, the mood was to change very abruptly.

In June of 1970, and without any warning, rival ERF made a takeover bid for the company which, due to its low valuation of Atkinson stock, was resoundingly rejected. However, when a second higher offer was put on the table by ERF, Atkinson shareholders hardly had time to think about it before an even higher bid was made by ERF's Sandbach arch rival, Foden.

Atkinson management and loyal operators mounted a campaign to fight off the offers, and disaster was averted when the ERF offer lapsed and the Foden offer was rejected. Eventually, Seddon stepped in with an offer the shareholders couldn't refuse, and at the end of 1970 the merger with Seddon was official.

Gardner 150-powered Atkinson Searcher.

Last of the breed ... the last true Atkinson rolled off the Walton-le-Dale production line in 1975, so this 1976-registered Rolls-Royce Eagle-powered Defender must have been one of the very last built.
(Courtesy Gyles Carpenter)

This extended-cab Venturer 6x4 sports a Gardner straight-eight 240bhp diesel, and probably started life as a heavy haulage tractor. (Courtesy Gyles Carpenter)

Twin-steer tractors, such as this Gardner 180-powered 6x2 Defender, were popular in the early 1970s, as a way of grossing 32 tonnes when hauling short trailers.
(Courtesy Gyles Carpenter)

In the late 1960s Atkinson attempted to modernise its trucks with the Viewline cab. However, few were built and most went to Pickfords Heavy Haulage.
(Courtesy Chris Gardner)

and SEDDON

Oldham-based Seddon entered the 1970s with a comprehensive range of light, medium, and heavyweight trucks, powered by an eclectic mix of Perkins, Gardner, Cummins and Rolls-Royce diesels. It also had a thriving bus and coach business, but had stopped building eight-wheel rigids during the previous decade. The old fibreglass truck cab had been replaced by a Motor Panels steel version during the late 1960s.

As a sign of the times, Seddon kept a watchful eye on the influx of foreign manufacturers, and formed a joint company with German engine maker Magirus Deutz, called Seddon Deutz. This enabled it to fit Deutz air-cooled engines into Seddon truck and bus chassis for export markets. It worked well technically, but sales were disappointing. Ultimately, the joint venture factory was sold to the German manufacturer, and used until it moved into larger dedicated premises in Winsford.

Much of the success of Seddon's heavyweight tractor units was due to the development of its own hub-reduction 13-ton rear axle, and, in 1970, the company was deemed to be the most productive and profitable independent truck maker in Britain.

Whilst the chairman of Atkinson subsequently resigned, following the company's acquisition by Seddon, followed by most of the directors, the engineering integration of the two companies went fairly smoothly, with economies of scale achieved for major units such as engines and gearboxes. However, both brands urgently needed a new cab, and a new design already in development made even more economic sense when spread across the two vehicle lines.

By the time the new Motor Panels cab finally appeared in 1975, US truck and agricultural group International Harvester (IH) had acquired the entire share capital of Seddon Atkinson following its initial acquisition of a 33 per cent stake. The resulting Seddon-Atkinson 400 series set new standards in UK truck design, and within a year had taken 20 per cent of the heavy truck market. It also heralded the end of the Seddon and Atkinson brands in their own right.

A year later, the 14-16-ton Seddon-Atkinson 200 series was launched, and radically for the UK-built truck, was powered by the high-revving IH D-358 134bhp engine, built in Germany. Developed from the former Seddon 14-four truck, it won the 'Truck of the Year' award in 1977. This was complemented by the 300 series six-wheeler, 24-tonner, using the IH DT-466 turbocharged engine producing 196bhp.

This Gardner-powered Seddon 34.Four sports a Motor Panels day cab. (Courtesy Gyles Carpenter)

Above: Perkins-powered Seddon 16-Four.
(Courtesy Gyles Carpenter)

The Seddon-Atkinson 400 was launched in 1975, and quickly captured 20 per cent of the heavy truck market.

Bedford

Bedford entered the 1970s with a rather staid product lineup, but that was soon to change. The first new model of 1970 was the M-type 4x4 launched as a medium mobility military four-tonner replacement for the R-type, which had given sterling service to the British Army since it was introduced in 1952.

The TK had been the quintessential light truck in the UK since its announcement in 1959, and, powered by four- and six-cylinder engines, it sold in its thousands, proving to be an extremely popular and versatile light and medium-weight truck. Available in both rigid and tractor form, it had been complemented in 1966 by a bigger brother, the KM. Aimed squarely at the 16-ton GVW market – the heaviest allowed at the time for two axle rigids – it had new underpinnings, and used a newly developed 466in^3, 7.6-litre, 135bhp diesel, but got a non-tilting cab adapted from the TK range.

The rigid version was supplemented by a 24-ton GVW tractor unit, the heaviest then produced by Bedford. Once this tractor unit had been developed, Bedford then had the basis for a heavier GVW tractor, but needed a more powerful engine.

With no suitable in-house engine available, Bedford found a suitable unit within its parent General Motors, and this resulted in the 1972 launch of the short-lived KM 32-tonner. Powered by a Detroit Diesel 6V-71 two-stroke 200bhp V6 engine, which barely met the 192bhp mandatory minimum requirement of 6bhp per ton, this buzzy Bedford had sales of less than 100

The Bedford TK sold in its thousands, with many having a second life in Mediterranean countries, such as this tipper in Malta. (Courtesy Dave Gothard)

This four-axle Bedford TK shows the lengths that some operators would go to for operation at higher gross weights. (Courtesy Len Rogers)

during its two-year production run, but it did serve as a test bed for the truck that was to follow. Many drivers found it hard to adjust to the power characteristics of the two-stroke diesel which had to be kept revving for best performance, and its cab was considered small for a top-of-the-range truck.

In 1974, Bedford and General Motors made a serious commitment to enter the European maximum

Ryder was one of the many rental fleets that put Bedford TMs into service during the 1970s.

weight arena with the brand new TM range. The first phase included tractor units rated at 32 tonnes, developed from the short-lived KM 32-tonner, and powered by the 216bhp version of the Detroit Diesel 6V-71 engine. These first TMs had the narrow standard D-type tilt cab, and were followed a year later by versions powered by Bedford's 8.2-litre four-stroke 500 series 151bhp inline six.

They were followed in 1976 by the top-of-the-range TM which was pitched at the 19-42-tonne GVW category. Powered by the Detroit Diesel 8V-71 two-stroker producing 296bhp, versions were available in rigid and tractor configurations, with the full width F-type cab and the optional H-type sleeper cab. The TM was also launched in Germany through GM's Opel network under the Bedford Blitz brand.

However, once again conservative British operators disliked the DD engine, especially the poor fuel consumption of the V6 version, and drivers found it hard to adapt to the high-revving characteristics of the engines. Sales were poor, and were probably not helped by trials carried out by BRS which pitted TM3250 tractor units fitted with the 6V-71 two-stroke engine, against Seddon and ERF tractor units fitted with Rolls-Royce and Cummins 220bhp diesels.

BRS found that performance was regarded as 'noticeably inferior' to Rolls- and Cummins-powered units, and fuel consumption was high, so BRS decided against adding TMs to its nationwide fleet.

BMC

With the decline of heavy industries in postwar Britain, the government strove to aid stricken areas by setting up new industries. The British Motor Corporation (BMC) moved to Bathgate, in Scotland, in 1961 to build tractors

and light trucks, and employed some 6000 people at its peak.

However, as major component manufacturers declined to move to Scotland, and local firms were deterred from entering the automotive industry by high tooling costs, BMC was somewhat isolated, and incurred massive road transport costs to and from the plant, which adversely affected its fortunes.

BMC had introduced its Austin and Morris FJ series 12.5 GVW trucks in 1964, and these were some of the first trucks built in the UK with a tilt cab. However, when BMC was absorbed into Leyland in

The BMC Mastiff 16-tonner was the mainstay of many UK haulage fleets throughout the 1970s. (Courtesy BCVM)

Left: The BMC Mastiff 24-tonner was a capable if basic truck. (Courtesy BCVM)

Bottom left: The BMC range was rebranded as Leyland Redline in 1970, and the Perkins 179bhp, V8-powered, 28-tonner was considered by many operators to be out of its depth at this weight. (Courtesy Richard Stanier)

1968, both the Austin and Morris names were dropped on heavy trucks, in favour of a single BMC brand, although this was relatively short-lived as the range was rebranded yet again as Leyland Redline in 1970.

The BMC-derived Leyland Mastiff was one of a number of pseudo heavyweights afflicted with the high-revving Perkins V8. Some operators believed that the truck was out of its depth at 24 tons, but at 32 tons it would have made driving conditions somewhat desperate.

Commer

Like many other British truck manufacturers, Commer rolled into the 1970s under the shadow of change. It had used its almost legendary horizontally-opposed, three-cylinder, six-piston, 3261cc, water-cooled and turbocharged 105bhp TS3 diesel, sometimes referred to as the 'Commer knocker' due to its unique noise, throughout the 1950s and '60s, but its days, along with the Commer brand, were numbered.

The Commando 100 series had been developed by Commer as a concept in 1965 as a replacement for the aging Commer VC range. However, when Commer's parent company, the Rootes Group, was acquired by Chrysler in 1967 following huge losses, and the commercial failure of the Hillman Imp car, the acquisition put Commer on a collision course with

Chrysler's other truck brand, Dodge, and its newly introduced Dodge 500 Series.

At the same time, the British Government was looking at introducing new legislation on power-to-weight ratios, and noise emissions. The noise legislation had a devastating effect on the future of Commer's TS3 and the more powerful TS4 in development, as neither engine could be economically suppressed to meet the new legislation.

Further complicating the issue was the fact that

The ageing VC range with Rootes two-stroke power soldiered on into the early 1970s, but was eventually replaced by the Commer Commando. (Courtesy Gyles Carpenter)

Above: The Commer Maxiload with the TS3 two-stroke diesel was a popular choice for many UK haulage firms. (Courtesy Richard Stanier)

Chrysler had invested millions of pounds in a UK joint venture with Cummins to produce new diesel engines (the disastrous Cummins VALE V6 and V8) and also had lucrative supplier agreements in place with Perkins for the supply of its 6.354 inline six-cylinder, and its new 185bhp 510in3 V8 diesel.

However, when Chrysler's management became aware of the extraordinary power-to-weight ratio, reliability, fuel efficiency, and low manufacturing costs of the 200bhp Commer TS4 engine, it knew it couldn't sell Dodge/Commer heavy trucks with the Cummins or Perkins V8s if it allowed the TS4 to reach production. The project cancelled and all prototypes, tooling and drawings were destroyed.

There was a great deal of rationalisation of the Dodge, Karrier and Commer ranges, and once the revamped Commando was released in 1974, the TS3 engine was phased out in favour of the Perkins 6.354. Chrysler also wanted to market the Commer nee Dodge 100 across Europe, and so standardised on Perkins diesels, and offered the 120bhp Mercedes-Benz OM 352 powerplant as a premium option in markets where Perkins was relatively unknown. It was sold across Europe under Commer, Dodge, DeSoto and Fargo brands, and, ultimately, as Renault.

The Commer named was phased out in 1976, with all former Commer models rebranded as Dodge. After Peugeot purchased Chrysler Europe in 1978, the former Commer factory was run in partnership with the truck division of Renault. It continued to produce the Dodge commercial truck range for some time, with Renault badges, and did a small amount of product development.

Dennis

Best known as a manufacturer of fire appliances, the Guildford-based firm also had a reputation of building high-quality buses, refuse collection vehicles, and even airport service vehicles.

The plastic-cabbed, medium-weight Pax was joined in 1964 by Dennis' fraught attempt to join the heavyweight market. Like Ford and Dodge, Dennis launched the Maxim range of heavyweight rigid and tractor units powered by the disastrous and short-lived Cummins Vale V8. A lightweight, 32-ton GVW tractor unit was launched, but the 185bhp Cummins unit was a sales flop. By 1967, the Maxim had to be re-engineered to accept the 170bhp Perkins V8 510, and was now rated at 30 tons GVW, yet still boasted a payload of 21 tons to rival that of five-axle 32-tonners.

However, neither version of the Maxim was a sales success and by the early 1970s Dennis had retreated to building light- and medium-weight trucks, with its Defiant tractor range powered by the turbocharged Perkins 155bhp straight-six.

Following financial difficulties, the company was acquired in 1972 by the Hestair Group and renamed Hestair Dennis. Hestair introduced a plan to upgrade the previous, virtually obsolete range, and pull out of the crowded UK transport market altogether. The company re-focussed on new fire engine technology and building trucks for vehicles for export, such as the Dominant and Defiant-based trucks assembled in Cyprus by the Kasis Motor Company (KMC), which in turn exported them to Greece, Libya and the Middle East.

As a result, the company finally recovered from huge losses, and ventured back into the bus market. Heartened by its export successes, Dennis commissioned a modified version of the Delta-2 chassis, and re-entered the UK domestic truck market in 1978.

KMC in Cyprus assembled a number of Dennis 16-tonners which were exported to Eastern Mediterranean and Middle Eastern countries. (Courtesy Richard Stanier)

Left: The Perkins-powered Dennis 16-tonner was a rare sight on UK roads in the 1970s. (Courtesy Gyles Carpenter)

Dennison

When Dennison sold its trailer business to Crane Fruehauf in 1975, the Dublin-based manufacturer had to abide by an agreement to stay out of trailer manufacturing for five years. However, that didn't stop the Irish firm from venturing into truck production.

George Dennison comments, "We started our truck project in 1976, and had the first two, a 6x4 tipper and a 4x2 tractor unit, ready for an official launch in June 1977. We built 250 from then until we ceased production in March 1981.

"The first 75 trucks had a Motor Panels base cab, and we constructed the front and inside sections with fibre glass. We then brought in 175 mixed day and sleeper cabs from Sisu in Finland. 200 Dennison trucks had Rolls-Royce Eagle engines; 50 had Gardners, and just four were fitted with Cummins. We fitted Eaton Fuller gearboxes, Eaton rear axles, and Kirkstall front axles.

"However, we were buying all of our parts, including the cab, in sterling, and when Ireland joined the EMS in March 1979 we lost 25 per cent of our buying power literally overnight. Whereas our competitors, such as

Volvo and Scania, etc, by being on the Continent didn't lose out at all.

"Also, the second oil crisis kicked in, and Maggie Thatcher came to power and the general economy in Ireland, the UK, went into decline. We ceased truck production in March 1981, just as the five years were up, and we went back to building trailers. However, closing the truck business proved very costly, and it cost us 1.3 million Irish punts to close it up."

Irish trailer maker Dennison ventured into truck production in 1976.

Dennison trucks were built between 1977-81, and most were fitted with Finnish-built Sisu cabs. (Courtesy Bill Reid)

Dodge

Development of the cab-forward Dodge K-series, latterly known as the 500 series, was begun in the early 1960s to take advantage of impending changes to UK Construction & Use regulation, which allowed for heavier gross vehicle weights. It was engineered at Dodge's Kew works, and fitted with a tilt cab designed by Ghia in Turin.

Designed for operation from 13-28 tonnes GVW, the new Dodges were somewhat radical in their use of the newly-developed, high-revving Cummins VALE V6 and V8 diesels built at Darlington under a 50/50 joint venture between Chrysler and Cummins. The 140bhp V6 revved to 3300rpm, whilst the 170bhp V8 peaked at 3000rpm; and they were noisy beasts. In the mid-1960s the author worked for a haulier which took delivery of a new V8-powered 16 tonner that could be heard returning to the depot whilst almost half a mile away.

Sadly, the reliability of the Cummins VALE engines was abysmal, and by early '69 Dodge had replaced it with the Perkins V8-510 in the heavyweight K1000 model instead.

The K-series 28-tonne tractor unit was designed around the ill-fated Cummins VALE V6 diesel, which proved to be both noisy and unreliable. (Courtesy John Ormandy)

This 24-tonne 6x4 has had an aftermarket second steering axle fitted to give it a gross weight of 28 tonnes. (Courtesy Richard Stanier)

This 6x4 Dodge tractor was operated in New Zealand at between 30-35 tonnes GVW with its original Cummins Vale V8. (Courtesy Trevor Jones)

The former Commer Commando was rebranded as the Dodge 100 and sold in a number of export markets. This example, seen in Finland, has a Valmet diesel, and what appears to be a locally-built sleep cab. (Courtesy Max Chern)

When the Commer brand was acquired by Chrysler in 1967, Dodge found itself in direct competition with its new stablemate. However, once the former Commer Commando became the Dodge 100, it perfectly complemented the heavier K-series Dodges. When Peugeot-Talbot took over the company from Chrysler in 1979, the heavyweight K-series was dropped the following year.

ERF

The 1970s really did start off with a bang for ERF. Record sales of £9.7 million were accompanied by the 1972 debut of the new A-Series truck, sporting fibreglass cabs from in-house coachbuilding firm JH Jennings. A modular design for mass production, the 34-ton GVW A-series tractor unit was offered with either Cummins or Gardner diesels, and a 38-ton European version was offered with a Motor Panels steel tilting cab.

Essentially an updated version of the previous LV series, the A-series was relatively short-lived, being superseded by the B-series introduced in 1974 with a steel-framed and plastic-panelled cab. This was the first production ERF to have a tilt cab, and was available in the normal 'day cab' configuration, and optional 'sleeper cab' versions – a very radical idea for British trucks in 1974.

Series production commenced mid way through 1975, with Gardner, Cummins and Rolls-Royce engine options. There was also a smaller M-series rigid with the walkthrough cab design. This looked much like the larger B-series, but had the headlamps in the bumper. Most were fitted with Gardner engines, although the Dorman V8 was listed as an option.

This A-series was a short-lived version of the previous LV series. This 24-tonner is powered by a Gardner 180.

Left: This Motor Panels steel cab was a popular option for ERFs exported to New Zealand, such as this eight-wheeler and drawbar livestock hauler. (Courtesy Rod Simmons)

Below: Sleeper cab version of the Motor Panels steel cab.

The ERF 38-tonne Eurotruck was launched in 1973, with an updated Motor Panels tilt cab. Gardner and Cummins engine options were available, although the NTC 335 proved popular in Europe. (Courtesy Rik Meeder)

ERF B-series cattle truck assembled from a CKD kit in New Zealand. (Courtesy Rod Simmons)

Day-cabbed B-series with Cummins power. (Courtesy Gyles Carpenter)

Foden

Foden entered 1970 in buoyant mood, but with an extensive range of 1960s trucks that needed simplifying to meet the changing needs of the 1970s. Surprisingly, when Atkinson was being subjected to a take-over bid by rival ERF in 1970, Foden launched its own, unsuccessful, bid.

The Sandbach-based truck maker gained a sales impetus in 1972 when the GVW on eight-wheelers was increased to 30 tons, and, in the same year, it launched the spacious S80 reinforced glass fibre tilt cab that was to become standard fitment on most models through the range. This was complemented by a Motor Panels cab option for operators requiring a steel cab.

In 1974, Foden introduced the 'Universal' range aimed at the European truck market, with models up to 100 tonnes GVW, and Cummins engines up to 355bhp. It featured the steel S90 Motor Panels cab, as fitted to its military range. However, despite the need to simplify its range, Foden proceeded to update the S80 cab to S83 spec, whilst introducing a number of half-cab options, as well as cabs with a 'snout' in order to fit the straight-eight Gardner 240.

Fleetmaster and Haulmaster models, developed from the Universal, were launched in 1977.

The Haulmaster was aimed at the UK market, used a Foden gearbox and axles, and was powered by a Cummins 250; whilst the Fleetmaster used a proprietary driveline, and had a choice of high-power Cummins or Rolls-Royce diesels. Both used a derivative of the S90 steel cab.

Foden 24-tonner with glass fibre S39 cab. (Courtesy Gyles Carpenter)

British manufacturers

The S50 half-cab first appeared in 1968 and proved popular with tipper operators. The cab even appeared on some artic units, which must have made it the ultimate day cab.

This Foden 8x2 rigid sports an S80 tilt cab.
(Courtesy Bill Clowes)

The Foden Fleetmaster was a development of the Haulmaster, and had a Fuller transmission and Rockwell rear axle. (Courtesy Bill Clowes)

The Foden Haulmaster tractor unit was aimed squarely at the UK market. It used Foden axles and gearbox, and a Cummins 250.

Ford

On its debut in 1965, the Ford D-series was a major departure from its predecessor, the Thames Trader. Its modern tilt cab was much more stylish than its main rival, the Bedford TK, and aimed at the light- and medium-weight market; it quickly won a devoted following.

Powered initially by in-house four- and six-cylinder diesels, the range was boosted in 1967 with the introduction of the D1000 heavyweight range. The 16-ton four-wheeler, 24-ton six-wheeler, and 28-ton GVW tractor units were initially powered by the short-lived Cummins Vale V8, before being re-engineered to accept the Perkins V8. The lightweight tractor unit could carry a full 20-ton load, even at 28 tons GVW, and paved the way for Ford's entry into the super-heavy league with the Ford Transcontinental.

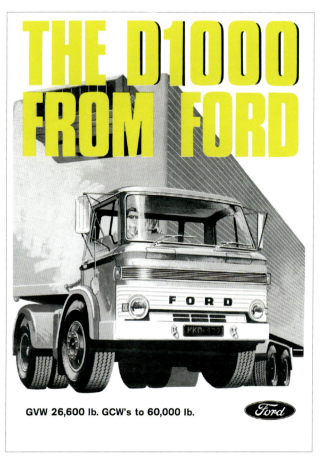

THE D1000 FROM FORD

GVW 26,600 lb. GCW's to 60,000 lb.

The D1000 was the top-of-the-range Ford truck in the late 1960s. Originally fitted with the ill-fated Cummins Vale V8, later versions had the Perkins V8. (Richard Stanier collection)

Ford D-series drawbar outfit. (Richard Stanier collection)

The Ford Transcontinental was launched in 1973 from Ford's plant in Amsterdam. (Courtesy Niles Jansen)

Using a chassis based on the successful L-series from the US, the Ford Transcontinental used a Berliet cab and proprietary running gear, such as Cummins engines, Fuller gearboxes, and Eaton axles. (Courtesy David Jaffrey)

Launched in 1973, the Ford H-series, or Transcontinental as is was to become known, was designed for operation at up to 42 metric tonnes GVW – the highest gross weight envisaged at the time. Developed at Ford's engineering facility at Dunton, in Essex, the new super heavyweight Ford would initially be assembled in Amsterdam, thus reinforcing Ford's plans to market it directly against established European truck makers.

Guy

Jaguar cars acquired ailing Guy Motors of Wolverhampton from the receiver in 1961, and the Guy Big J (Big Jaguar) was launched just three years later. Designed initially with a tilting Motor Panels cab, the tilting mechanism was deleted when series production commenced in 1966 to save cost.

Like the Ford D1000 and Dodge K-series, the Big J was initially designed around the disastrous high-revving Cummins Vale V6. However, it had to be redesigned in short order to accept reliable inline sixes from AEC, Gardner, Leyland, Perkins, and Rolls-Royce.

The revised truck sold so well that, even after being absorbed into the Leyland camp in 1968, the Wolverhampton firm continued to build trucks at an average rate of 9-10 per week, despite Leyland's desire to consign the brand to the scrapheap along with AEC, Albion, and Scammell.

However, lack of investment in an old and dilapidated factory, machinery, and the truck itself, meant that the last Big J rolled out of the Fallings Park plant on 2 February 1979, after more than 16,000 had been built.

A large order book for Guy Victory buses kept the plant partially occupied, and spare capacity was taken up by assembling Scammell Crusaders from parts shipped up from the Tolpits Lane factory. A small number of Leyland Marathons were also assembled at the Guy plant, as were Leyland T43 Landtrains, before production of these was switched to Leyland's Bathgate factory, resulting in the closure of the Wolverhampton factory in August 1982 with the loss of 740 jobs.

The Guy Big J (Big Jaguar) was originally designed with a tilting cab. However, production models got a fixed version. (Courtesy BCVM)

The Big J cab fitting-out line at Wolverhampton. (Courtesy BCVM)

The Guy Big J was a popular truck with tank haulage firms such as Pickfords. (Courtesy BCVM)

The Big J proved popular with tipper operators, too. (Courtesy BCVM)

This unusual Big J has a sleep cab conversion, and wasn't registered until 1984: long after production had ceased.

The Big J proved popular with general haulage contractors, such as BRS. (Courtesy Bill Clowes)

Leyland

The Leyland Truck & Bus division began the 1970s reeling from the financial burden imposed on it by the ailing car manufacturers brought into the group, following the merger with BMC in 1968. All of the truck manufacturers within the group had been both healthy and profitable, but as profits were siphoned off to keep loss-making car brands afloat, the truck business suffered from a catastrophic lack of investment.

"British Leyland squandered the profits from successful truck makers to develop and build cars, such as the disastrous Austin Allegro," said former Leyland Truck & Bus communications director, Martin Hayes. "As a result, the truck side of the business was forced to rely on its reputation instead of new products.

"Eventually, truck export markets started to collapse, and with the construction of motorways in the UK, high-powered Volvos and Scanias quickly became the trucks of choice for long distance trucking, having already been designed to ply the high speed autobahns of Germany.

"By the time that Leyland realised it needed to establish itself across Europe, as an island-only market could not sustain it, the ailing car divisions had already swallowed up most of the funds from the truck makers, and now it was just too expensive to get into Europe.

"Sadly, it was a case of too little too late, and the investment which led to the Roadtrain (and later the Roadrunner), the Leyland Assembly Plant, and the associated Leyland Technical Centre was not enough. Own goals, like the advanced but initially catastrophically unreliable 500 engine, didn't help either," concluded Hayes.

British Leyland had entered the 1970s with a large number of competing brands and products, not least those actually badged as Leylands. The former BMC trucks were now badged as Leyland Redline, whilst the 'official' Leylands were badged as Leyland Blueline. And then there were the former Albions, which were also now badged as Leylands. As components, engines and cabs were shared across many of the models, it must have been a truly confusing time for operators.

The ergo-cabbed Leyland Comet-Badger-Hippo-Beaver range was phased out in 1971 to make way for the new-improved Buffalo, Bison and Lynx range. These featured face-lifted, high-datum versions of the ergo cab, and were powered by the infamous Leyland

The last of the breed ... the heavyweight Hippo 6x4 was
phased out in 1971. (Courtesy BCVM)

This Leyland Boxer was one of the former BMC models
re-badged as part of the Leyland Redline range.

In 1972, the former Albion range was also re-badged as Leyland, with G-cabs from the Leyland Redline range.
(Courtesy BCVM)

Top left: The lightweight Leyland Bear was not a popular addition to the Lynx/Buffalo range. (Courtesy BCVM)

Top right: The Leyland Marathon, introduced in 1973, was intended as a serious contender in the transcontinental super heavyweight league. (Courtesy BCVM)

Left: Unfortunately, the Marathon looked like it had been cobbled together from leftover Ergomatic cab parts, and the AEC-built TL12 turbo-diesel, although powerful enough, had teething problems. (Courtesy BCVM)

500 fixed-head engine. Developed as something of a knee jerk reaction to head gasket failures on Leyland's ubiquitous 680 unit, the new engine suffered from poor build quality, which led to engine seizures and appalling durability and reliability. Within six years, Leyland announced that it would phase out the engine.

AEC was forced to soldier on with the old-style ergo cab as Leyland chiefs refused it access to the new high-datum unit. Plans to re-engineer the under-developed AEC V8 engine were shelved whilst Leyland coffers were squandered on the 500 unit, and the Buffalo quickly developed a reputation for such poor reliability that it was ultimately one of the nails in Leyland's coffin. Even versions powered firstly by the L12 version of the old AEC AV790 and then the TL11 – a turbocharged development of the old Leyland 680 unit – failed to win over operators. Perhaps if Leyland had installed Gardner, Cummins or Rolls-Royce diesels, instead of focussing exclusively on in-house engines, things might have worked out differently.

So, whilst the likes of the Buffalo, Mandator and Big J catered for heavyweight requirements, behind the scenes Leyland was also trying to develop a super-heavyweight truck designed for long-haul work, and capable of taking on the best truck in Europe. However, the T25 project, which ultimately turned into the Leyland Marathon, came a poor second to the likes of Mercedes-Benz, Scania, and Volvo long-haul cruisers.

Launched in 1973, with a cab looking like it had been cobbled together from leftover ergo parts, and a modified AEC six-cylinder engine developing 286bhp, the Marathon never really lived up to expectations. Designed and built at Leyland's (AEC) Southall plant, the Marathon suffered from a lack of investment and under-development.

BRS, then Britain's biggest road haulage firm, tested two Marathons, and reported cracked pistons on the TL12 in under a year. Despite Cummins and Rolls-Royce engines being available for export markets, it wasn't until 1976 that they became available in UK spec trucks, by which time Leyland's reputation had been badly tarnished, compounded by the ill-fated 500-series engine debacle.

When the AEC plant was finally closed in 1979, Leyland transferred production of the Marathon to Scammell's Watford plant to take up some of the spare capacity caused by the phasing out of the Crusader. Some Marathons were even built off-line at Guy's Wolverhampton plant, and whilst AEC and Guy were heading for the scrapheap, Leyland focussed on its next generation of trucks, the T45 range, but that's another story.

Scammell

The Watford-based truck maker carved out a name for itself in such fields as heavy construction, oil drilling, mining and logging, as well as maintaining a healthy military presence. Its acquisition by Leyland in 1955 gave it ready access to Leyland driveline components, and the Michelotti-designed 'cheese-grater' glass fibre reinforced plastic cab for the Routeman, Handyman, and 6x2 Trunker tractor enabled Scammell to make steady inroads into the haulage market.

However, despite its Leyland ownership, Scammell had a virtual free hand in building trucks to its own design, which meant that it didn't get lumbered with the Ergomatic cab that graced AEC, Albion and Leyland trucks in the mid-1960s. Following the buzz about the possibility of increased gross vehicle weights in the late 1960s, and the rumours of 44 tonnes being allowed with a 6x4 tractor, Scammell decided to fly the flag for Leyland and design and build its own 44-tonne model.

A prototype, powered by the ill-fated AEC V8, resulted in the production Scammell Crusader 6x4, which was unveiled in 1969 and looked more like an American truck than anything seen previously on British roads – with twin exhaust stacks and a replacement two-stroke Detroit Diesel 8V71 motor under its chunky, although basic, Motor Panel cab. Although developed as a knee-jerk reaction to an ill-founded rumour of an increase in permissible weights, the Crusader proved popular in export markets and with Britain's military chiefs, who ordered some 500 in various forms.

The Scammell Routeman first made its appearance in 1962, with its Michelotti-designed 'cheese grater' cab. It progressed from 8x2 to 8x4 for the Mk III model, which was rated at 26 tonnes GVW. (Courtesy BCVM)

British manufacturers

The 6x2 twin-steer Trunker was developed to pull short trailers at the maximum 32 tonnes GVW. Leyland- and Gardner-powered versions proved extremely popular with fuel companies.

The Handyman 4x2 first appeared in 1964 and, despite being available in day cab form only, was still a volume seller well into the early 1970s. (Courtesy BCVM)

Prototype Scammell Contractor for the army undergoing deep water testing. (Courtesy BCVM)

Super-heavyweight Contractor tank transporter. (Courtesy Len Rogers)

Scammell entered the 1970s with the most diverse range of trucks in the British Leyland portfolio. A wide range of on- and off-highway trucks was complemented by the massive Scammell Contractor, a heavy haulage tractor capable of a 240-tonne gross train weight.

Pressure from BRS saw the introduction of a Rolls-Royce Eagle-powered 4x2 version of the Crusader. In fact, these later versions become so popular that production was transferred to the Guy Motors Wolverhampton plant to take up the capacity left by the demise of the Big J.

At the same time, the closure of Thornycroft in 1972 resulted in the transfer of the 'Nubian' range of 6x6 airfield crash tenders to Scammell, together with the AEC LD55 6x4 dump truck; both rebranded as Scammell.

A surge of development in the late 1970s commenced with the Contractor Mk II heavy hauler, with its 18-litre, 425hp Cummins KT450 engine and Allison automatic gearbox, developed from a design initiated by heavy haulage firm Wynns of Newport.

Scammell also developed the Commander Tank Transporter for the British Army. This 100-ton+ GTW tractor, fitted with the Rolls-Royce CV12TCE 26-litre, 48-valve, dual-turbocharged, 625hp, intercooled V12 diesel engine, semi-automatic gearbox and Scammell 40-ton bogie, was required to have the same acceleration and braking performance as a contemporary 32-tonner!

Whilst Scammell managed to avoid the fate that had befallen AEC, Albion, Guy, and Thornycroft during the

The Scammell Crusader was designed to take the ill-fated AEC V8. However, problems with the engine in the prototype saw it hastily removed and substituted by the Detroit Diesel two-stroke 8V71 instead. (Courtesy BCVM)

Designed initially for operation at the proposed 44-tonne GVW limit, the Crusader pipped all other Leyland group firms for the biggest and baddest truck. (Courtesy BCVM)

In 1971 Scammell launched the 8x4 Sampson, with a 290bhp Detroit Diesel two-stroke and a GVW of 75 tonnes. The only example built went to Pickfords Heavy Haulage, where it was soon discovered that a standard 6x4 Crusader could easily move the same gross weight. (Courtesy BCVM)

British manufacturers

Wynns was a big customer of heavyweight Scammells, and this Rolls-Royce Eagle-powered 6x4 could handle up to 100 tonnes GVW.

Following pressure from BRS, Scammell introduced a Rolls-Royce-powered 4x2 Crusader. (Courtesy BCVM)

1970s, the following decade would see the Leyland bean-counters finally focus on the Tolpits Lane plant.

Shelvoke & Drewry

The Letchworth-based firm entered the 1970s as a leading supplier of specialist vehicles to local authorities. Refuse collection, drain cleaning, and septic tank emptying were popular use for S&D-based trucks, and the 1971 introduction of the Revopak had enabled the company to increase its UK market share to 66 per cent.

The N-type, with a Motor Panels steel cab, was introduced in 1972, and, following the sale of its fork-lift truck business in 1975, S&D used the vacant space to launch its Special Purpose Vehicle (SPV) Division. This new division worked in conjunction with Carmichael to build and design a range of fire appliances which quickly won major orders from many UK fire services.

Shelvoke introduced the Special Purpose Vehicle (SPV) range in 1975. (Courtesy Richard Stanier)

Thornycroft

By this time, divisional reorganisation within the Leyland Group had resulted in the firm's name becoming Scammell Motors, and the closure of Transport Equipment (Thornycroft) in 1972 had resulted in the transfer of its 'Nubian' range of 6x6 airfield crash tenders to Scammell, together with the LD55 6x4 dumptruck.

Unipower

Third axle conversions and the construction of 4x4 timber haulage tractors had helped the Perivale, West London-based company develop a healthy niche market. However, production of the timber tractors was axed at the start of the decade, and the company focussed on production of the Invader truck and numerous multi-axle conversions on Commers, Dodges and Fords.

The Unipower Invader 4x4 was developed as a cross between a Seddon 16-Four fitted with an AEC front axle. (Courtesy Richard Stanier)

European manufacturers

Astra

Founded in Italy in 1946 as the Azienda Sarda Trasformazione Autoveicoli, the Astra workshop refurbished former military vehicles left behind at the end of WWII, and adapted them for civilian use.

In 1951, Astra moved to the city of Piacenza, in the same region where the likes of Ferrari, Maserati, Lamborghini and Ducati were based, and in just four years the company had designed and built its first quarry dump truck. During the 1970s it added crane chassis to its product range.

Astra 6x6 with Fiat cab. (Courtesy Len Rogers)

Barreiros

The Chrysler Corporation took control of Spanish truck maker Barreiros Diesel in 1969, and the following year the company was renamed Chrysler España SA. Barreiros was essentially a builder of heavy trucks, and it entered the UK truck market at the end of 1973 with its K3820P tractor unit designed for operation at 38 tonnes GVW, and badged as Dodge.

Initially powered by an 11.9-litre, 270bhp, turbocharged Chrysler power unit, the truck was quickly revised as the Dodge 300 series, with a sleeper cab and Cummins diesel options.

The company continued constructing trucks under the name Barreiros in Spain until 1978, whereupon it was changed to Dodge España when Chrysler Europe

After Chrysler took control of Barreiros, its heavyweight trucks were badged as Dodge. (Courtesy Lex Meeder)

was bought out by Peugeot. The company and factory was passed over to Renault in 1981.

Berliet

With a history of building everything from armoured personnel carriers for the military to mighty 600bhp desert terrain trucks for oilfield exploration, the French truck maker was taken over by Citroën in 1967 – Citroën itself having been owned by Michelin since 1934.

Berliet entered the UK truck market in 1971, with its dumpy TR250 tractor, but within a year had introduced its stylish TR280 tractor unit rated at 38 tonnes GVW, and a bonneted GBH 280 6x4 off-road tipper. The TR280 was powered by a 12-litre, 242bhp, six-cylinder diesel, and, for TIR and Middle East operations, a TR320

38-tonner was also available, fitted with a 15-litre, 301bhp V8 diesel.

Following the 1973 oil crisis, Michelin decided to divest itself of these two companies in order to concentrate wholly on its tyre business. Michelin had prolonged negotiations with Volvo, but the Swedish manufacturer was only interested in a merger which would enable it to build Volvos in France, and had no real interest in Berliet trucks. Thus, in 1974, Berliet was sold to Renault, while Citroën was sold to Peugeot. Renault then proceeded to merge Berliet with Saviem to form Renault Vehicules Industriels (RVI).

This bonneted 6x4 Berliet is shown here hauling a 150-tonne load in Portugal. Great 'old school' ballast box!
(Courtesy Rik Meeder)

The 'Relaxe' steel cab was introduced in 1959, and was used on all forward control Berliet heavyweights until 1971. (Courtesy Len Rogers)

Berliet introduced its new range of trucks with stylish new cabs in 1971. This TRH350 featured the top-of-the-range 350bhp V8. (Courtesy Niels Jansen)

By 1975, RVI had begun phasing out the Berliet name, and, by the end of the decade another French marque had come to a sad end.

Berna

Berna was a Swiss company manufacturing buses, trolleybuses and trucks, which was then taken over by rival Saurer. In the early 1950s, Saurer reached an agreement with Italian truck builder OM under which Saurer would market light- and medium-weight Italian-built trucks and buses using Saurer-OM and Berna-OM badges.

Vehicle manufacturing was taken over completely by Saurer in 1978, and the Berna name was discontinued. (Courtesy Len Roger)

Büssing

German truck builder Büssing's speciality was the development of the underfloor-engined truck.

In 1969, Büssing developed strong ties with MAN, resulting in a take-over of Büssing in 1971, the same year that it attempted to enter the UK truck market via Yorkshire-based truck dealer Brian Watt Commercials.

However, following the takeover by MAN, the company's trucks were re-badged as MAN-Büssing,

and, within two years had become something of a hybrid, using MAN chassis and cab, whilst the horizontal underfloor engine layout incorporated a new D25 six-cylinder, 256bhp engine developed in conjunction with Daimler Benz.

Büssing's unique underfloor-engined truck range continued in production under MAN AG through to the late 1980s.

Büssing was taken over by MAN in 1971.
(Courtesy Rik Meeder)

DAC

DAC trucks were produced by Autocamioane Brasov, the same Romanian company that manufactured ROMAN trucks. They also featured the same Saviem-designed cab.

DAF

The 1970s heralded a whole new era for Dutch truck maker DAF, with new trucks, new engines, new markets, new partners, and, most importantly, new management. The old-style bonneted trucks had been phased out, and 1970 saw the launch of the brand new modular tilt cab, first introduced in the 1600 and 2000 series, but eventually in the flagship 2800 series which, in itself, replaced the trendsetting 2600 series.

Whilst the Eindhoven-based firm had been busy upgrading, developing and turbocharging the old Leyland 350 and 680 engines it had originally built under licence, it kicked off the 1970s with a brand new mid-range DH825 engine producing 218bhp in turbocharged form.

In 1972, the firm set up DAF Trucks UK, and, whilst it was one of the last European truck builders to enter the UK, the quality of its dealer network and aftersales service saw it make a long-lasting impression on UK truck operators and fleets. In 1973, International Harvester acquired a 33 per cent stake in the company, following near disastrous attempts to break into the European truck market under its own brand, and this led to some interesting hybrids.

In 1979, DAF finally joined the growing number of European truck makers that had launched 8x4 chassis

DAF 6x6 trucks proved popular in the construction industry. (Courtesy Rik Meeder)

The DAF F2800 series was introduced in 1974 as the flagship of the range. The 320bhp turbocharged and intercooled version proved popular with heavy haulage firms in the UK and across Europe.

to compete against home-grown products in the UK construction sector.

Ebro

Motor Iberica was set up in 1954 to build British-designed Ford trucks under licence. The first trucks built were versions of the Ford Thames, and so were named Ebro after a Spanish river. By the 1970s the trucks featured Perkins engines and a Spanish version of the D-series tilt cab in light- and medium-weight models up to 27 tonnes GVW.

FAP

Fabrika Automobila Priboj (FAP) is a Serbian manufacturer of trucks and buses. Founded in 1953, the company enjoyed a long-standing relationship with Mercedes-Benz, which provided engines and licenses for many of FAP's vehicles.

Serbian-built FAPs were licence-built Mercedes-Benz trucks. (Courtesy Juraj Hlavac)

Above: Ebro used a locally-built version of the Ford D-series cab. (Courtesy Rik Meeder)

57

Faun

Bavarian truck maker, FAUN GmbH entered the 1970s as a well-respected builder of road sweepers, dump trucks, foundry vehicles, and crane carriers, and quickly expanded into building airport fire trucks, tank transporters, and some memorable and truly massive heavy haulage tractors.

Right: The most memorable of all Faun trucks were the heavy haulage tractors. (Courtesy Ralf Koch)

Faun was primarily a builder of specialist vehicles, so this long-haul highway truck is something of a rarity. (Courtesy Niels Jansen)

FBW

Franz Brozincevic & Cie (FBW) was a Swiss maker of trucks and buses, active between 1922 and 1985, and based in Wetzikon.

FBW gained an excellent reputation for top-level engineering and long-lasting products, never producing series, but instead making individually-tailored vehicles. It used only components of its own manufacture – a costly system that allowed the company to produce only a few hundred units per year.

FBW built high-quality, individually-tailored vehicles.
(Courtesy Rik Meeder)

Fiat

With international regulations calling for higher cab strengths and the massive growth in long-haul TIR operations, truck operators were increasingly looking for larger sleeping cabs. This led Italian truck manufacturer Fiat to introduce a brand new pressed steel cab, which was fitted to all heavyweight Fiats, OMs and French UNIC trucks for the first time.

In 1972, Fiat announced it was entering the UK truck market with the 32-ton, 200bhp 684 and the heavier 38-ton, 260bhp 619 range, along with the 6x4 697 derivative. Non-tilting cabs were standard.

Fiat's association with Citroën, signed in 1968 to develop a series of lightweight trucks, had not been successful, so was dissolved in 1973, and the Italian firm looked around for more productive partners. A year later it concluded a deal with Klöckner Humbolt Deutz, whereby the German Magirus-Deutz truckmaking division (but not its engine manufacturing facility) would become part of a new Fiat-led group. It was joined by Fiat-owned UNIC from France, and the new conglomerate, named the Industrial Vehicles Corporation, abbreviated to IVECO, was officially announced in 1975.

However, neither Magirus nor UNIC was a profitable concern, and both OM and Fiat had a model range going back 20 years. So, for 1975, IVECO cut the Fiat/OM range in half and introduced the V8-powered, 17-litre, non-turbocharged, 352bhp 170/190 long-haul range, this time with a tilt cab.

Left: Turbocharged
V8-powered Fiat 190.
(Courtesy Rik Meeder)

IVECO introduced the V8-
powered Fiat 170 in 1975.
(Courtesy Lex Meeder)

FTF

Floor's Handel en Industrie, better known as FTF, started life as a Dutch haulage company that moved into the production of trailers in the 1950s. This was followed by importing and assembling Mack trucks for the Dutch market, but when Mack decided to set up its own operation in 1964, the new factory Floor had built to assemble Macks was put to use building its own Dutch-designed trucks. Initially, left-over Mack engines and components were used, but eventually FTF started installing Detroit Diesel two-strokes.

Cabs, similar to those used on Seddons and Guy Big Js, were sourced from Motor Panels in the UK, along with a choice of Allison or Fuller transmission and Rockwell or Kirkstall axles. Initially, production was centred on the heavy haulage market, but as the company's reputation grew it expanded into the production of regular haulage trucks.

FTF initially concentrated on building heavy haulage tractors powered by Detroit Diesels. (Courtesy Lex Meeder)

As FTF's reputation grew it expanded into general haulage trucks. (Courtesy Niels Jansen)

GINAF

Dutch specialist truck builder GINAF started refurbishing ex US Army REO 6x6s into dump trucks in the 1960s, and managed to carve out a healthy niche market. It installed DAF diesels, and then as sales increased became certified as a truck builder in its own right, using DAF axles and modified cabs. Because of this, GINAF trucks often look like modified DAFs, but underneath the chassis and running gear are all sourced by GINAF.

The company specialised in building on-off highway vehicles for the construction and agricultural sectors, as well as undertaking a number of specialist modifications to DAF trucks.

GINAF started out refurbishing ex-US army trucks, and eventually became a truck manufacturer in its own right.
(Courtesy Niels Jansen)

Henschel

In 1968, German truck manufacturer Henschel merged with Hanomag – which, at that time, mainly built lightweight vehicles – to form Hanomag-Henschel. It produced an innovative range of modular trucks, both in conventional and cab-over-engine configurations.

In 1970, Mercedes-Benz took control of the company and, shortly afterwards, started installing its own engines and axles into the heavyweight trucks. The last Hanomag-Henschel heavy truck rolled out of the

Hanomag Henschel H61 6x6. (Courtesy Niels Jansen)

Hanomag Henschel F261 6x6. (Courtesy Niels Jansen)

Kassel plant in 1974, by which time they were wearing the three-pointed star.

IFA

Industrieverband Fahrzeugbau ('Industrial Association for Vehicle Construction'), usually abbreviated as IFA, was a conglomerate and a union of companies for vehicle construction in the former East Germany (DDR). In addition to the manufacture of heavy trucks, IFA also produced such vehicles as the Trabant, Wartburg, and Barkas.

IFA W50L. (Courtesy Juraj Hlavac)

Jelcz

Polish truck maker Jelcz had a relatively short history compared with many of the old-established firms. Following a decision to use a former German armaments factory in Jelcz-Laskowice near Oława for vehicle production, a company called 'Zakłady Budowy Nadwozi Samochodowych' (factory for building car bodies) was established to build both Jelcz and Star trucks.

The heaviest trucks in the Jelcz range used a licence-built Leyland 680 engine, some of which ventured across Europe as long-haul international trucking operations grew. The dated-looking Jelcz cab was replaced in 1978 with a more modern-looking version.

Jelcz 312 from the early 1970s. (Courtesy Juraj Hlavac)

In 1978, Jelcz used a more modern cab, as fitted to this W642. (Courtesy Juraj Hlavac)

Kaelble

In postwar Germany, Kaelble carved out a niche market for its range of construction trucks and all-wheel-drive heavy road locomotives. Whilst it had been making general haulage trucks in Germany since the 1950s, Kaelble ceased production of these in 1973. It did, however, continue building crane carriers and fire-fighting equipment, and some truly monstrous heavy haulage tractors, for Deutsche Bahn (German Railways).

At the beginning of the 1970s, Kaelble also decided to pull the plug on engine building, and switch to proprietary units from the likes of Magirus-Deutz or Mercedes. By the end of the 1970s, the crane carrier range comprised 6x6, 8x4, 10x6, 12x8, and even 14x8 models, with engines of up to 1100bhp. Dump trucks now had 6- or 10-cylinder diesels of between 265 and 475bhp, and payload ratings of up to 35 tons, while a new range of articulated liquid slag haulers could cope with loads of up to 150 tons.

In 1976, the company merged with Gmeinder, and, in 1979, Kaelble Gmeinder was acquired by the Libyan company Lafico, which became the principal client of the company's trucks in an ill-fated venture.

LIAZ

LIAZ (LIberecké Automobilové Závody) was originally a division of Skoda, the Czechoslovak manufacturer of trucks, but became independent in 1953 (although it continued to use the Skoda Liaz name). In the 1970s, LIAZ was the biggest Czechoslovak truck manufacturer, and produced many heavyweight trucks for state-owned trucking outfit CSAD.

LIAZ 4x4. (Courtesy Juraj Hlavac)

LIAZ trucks were a popular choice for state-owned trucking outfit CSAD. (Courtesy Rik Meeder)

Magirus-Deutz

Magirus-Deutz entered the 1970s with a reputation based on air-cooled diesels ranging from V6, V8, V10 and right up to a 17-litre 340bhp V12. Keen to expand its market share in the lightweight trucks market, in 1971 it joined with Volvo, Saviem and DAF in the 'Club of Four' project to design and build lightweight trucks with a common cab design for all 'Club' members.

Following reasonable market penetration in the UK it built a brand new facility in Winsford, Cheshire, in 1972, which became the administrative headquarters of Magirus-Deutz (Great Britain) Ltd. At these facilities vehicles and parts were received from Germany and Italy, and distributed through a network of sales and service dealers all over the UK.

However, sales in the UK did not live up to expectations, and the following year rumours that

Klockner-Humbolt-Deutz, the parent company of Magirus, was looking for a buyer led to speculation that British Leyland, which was in dire need of a European extension of its truck and bus servicing network, might be a potential buyer. However, whilst the rumours never led to a deal with Leyland, the formation of The Industrial Vehicle Corporation (IVECO) in 1975 saw Magirus-Deutz joining forces with UNIC, Fiat Trucks, OM and Lancia Special Vehicles.

Over the next few years model and engine integration took place across the IVECO range and, in 1976, the first bonneted Magirus trucks appeared, with water-cooled FIAT diesels instead of the traditional Deutz air-cooled V8.

The air-cooled Deutz V8 proved extremely popular in the construction industry. (Courtesy Roland Sparling)

Looks like this Magirus tanker has lost traction and is causing traffic chaos in this snow-bound British town.
(Courtesy Les Freathy)

MAN

Maschinenfabrik Augsburg-Nürnberg (MAN) began truck production in Germany in 1915 following an ill-fated joint venture with Swiss-based Saurer.

The company was very astute in allowing other truck makers to build its products under licence, and in 1963 MAN entered into a cooperation agreement with Renault subsidiary Saviem, in order to add a selection of lightweight trucks to its range. The partnership produced a new modern cab, which MAN in turn provided to a number of other manufacturers, particularly in the former Eastern Bloc countries. The partnership with Renault lasted until 1977.

In 1971, MAN acquired German rival Büssing, and stepped up its activities in Austria by entering into a partnership agreement with ÖAF Gräf & Stift, which was well-known for its buses, all-wheel drive, and special purpose trucks.

Following the end of cooperation with Saviem. MAN looked for a new partner to build lightweight trucks, and found a willing partner in Volkswagen. This partnership resulted in a new range of lightweight MAN-VW trucks up to nine tonnes GVW.

In 1978, a MAN 19.280 won the coveted title of 'Truck of the Year,' and finally the company had vehicles to compete with the very best in Europe.

MAN 26.240 6x6 dump truck. (Courtesy Niels Jansen)

The 320bhp diesel in the super-heavyweight MAN 30.320 made it extremely popular with heavy haulage operators. (Courtesy Lex Meeder)

Mercedes-Benz

The brand new Mercedes-Benz 1.5 million square metre Wörth truck plant on the River Rhine delivered its first truck, an LP 608, in 1965, and this was the forerunner of the LP series that was to remain in production for the next 20 years. The cab-over LP series ushered in the end of the familiar bonneted truck range, and would help the plant quickly become the largest truck building facility in Europe – building more than 500,000 trucks within the first ten years of operation.

Mercedes had swallowed up German rival Hanomag-Henschell in 1970, but set a new bench mark in truck design with the 1973 introduction of the 'New

This bonneted MB 1418 double-trailer outfit operated in New Zealand. (Courtesy Trevor Jones)

Generation' range – stylish, aerodynamic cabs, and a new range of non-turbocharged 256bhp V8, and 320bhp V10 diesels. The latter, the 15.95-litre OM403 series, was introduced initially in anticipation of impending German legislation requiring a minimum of 8bhp per tonne for operation at 38 tonnes GVW. However, despite the legislation not actually being introduced, the powerhouse V10 proved so popular with long-haul operators that it quickly achieved almost legendary status in Europe.

The LP series was to remain in production for 20 years. (Courtesy F Michel)

Some of the most memorable trucks built by MOL in the 1970s were heavily modified, ex-British Army, Thornycroft Mighty Antar tank transporter tractors. Reconstructed as heavy haulage tractors complete with Deutz V12 diesels, MOL gave extended life to some of Basingstoke's finest. (Courtesy Rik Meeder)

The 'New Generation' of MB trucks was launched in 1973, and the top-of-the-range 320bhp V10-powered trucks proved popular with heavy haulage firms across Europe. (Courtesy Rik Meeder)

MOL

The Belgian MOL company was first formed in 1952, and built trucks under its own name from 1966 onwards. Specialising in on-off road, construction, oilfield and heavy haulage tractors, the company mostly used Magirus-Deutz air-cooled diesels, although Cummins and GM engines were also offered during the 1970s.

ÖAF

ÖAF are the initials of Österreichische Automobil-Fabrik, an Austrian truck builder in which MAN held a majority share since the 1930s.

In 1970, the company was privatised again, and MAN then let it merge with Gräf & Stift, out of which rose ÖAF Gräf & Stift, which, a year later, was acquired by MAN. The company was an experienced builder of specialist and multi-axle-driven trucks, and quickly became the specialist vehicle division of MAN, with most retaining an ÖAF grille.

OAF 32.320 6x4 on trial in Russia in the 1970s. (Courtesy Max Chern)

OM

Officine Meccaniche (OM) was an Italian-based manufacturer of light- and medium-weight trucks which was absorbed into the Fiat Group in 1968. However, its lifespan under Fiat was relatively short-lived as, in 1978, it was absorbed (as part of the Fiat Group) into IVECO, at which time the brand name on trucks was discontinued.

OM was absorbed into IVECO and the brand disappeared in 1978. (Courtesy Rik Meeder)

Pegaso

Pegaso was part of the Spanish state-owned ENASA company, which had interests in the truck and bus market. It focused mainly on the heavier end of the truck market, and built a wide variety of multi-axle highway, off-road, and military vehicles.

In 1972, Pegaso launched a new range of trucks featuring the Aldo Sessano-designed 'cubic' cab. The 2080 series featured a 10.5-litre 250bhp engine as standard, and a 12-litre 310bhp option when the 2181 series tilt cab was introduced in 1975.

Pegaso built more than 350,000 vehicles; the highest production in a single year was when it built more than 26,000 trucks in 1974.

Praga

As the name implies, Praga was a truck manufacturer based in Prague, in the Czech Republic.

The Praga V3S 6x6 range was introduced in 1952, primarily as a go-anywhere vehicle, and remained in production right through the 1970s. It was powered by a 7.4-litre, air-cooled, inline six, based on half of a Tatra V12 diesel from the T111 range. It was supplemented by the 5ST 4x2 which was aimed more at the civilian market.

The Praga V3S 6x6 range was introduced in 1952, primarily as a go-anywhere vehicle, and remained in production right through the 1970s. (Courtesy Juraj Hlavac)

Pegaso launched the cubic-cabbed 2080 series in 1975. (Courtesy Len Rogers)

RABA

The Hungarian Railway Carriage and Machine Works in Gyor had built RABA-branded trucks under licence from both Krupp and MAN prior to WWII. After the cessation of hostilities in Europe, the Soviets hived off many of the former RABA products to other Eastern Bloc plants, leaving Gyor to produce just axles, steering gear, and transmissions.

However, following the purchase of a new engine manufacturing licence from MAN in 1967, RABA quickly got back into truck manufacturing, and, by 1971, was able to launch its first long-haul trucks. Designed to operate at gross weights up to 38 tonnes, the new trucks were powered by RABA-MAN 215bhp or optional 230bhp diesels. These engines were older technology units, similar to those being built under licence by ROMAN and also supplied to Saviem. The trucks were also fitted with the generic Saviem-MAN cab.

RABA launched its first long-haul trucks in 1971. (Courtesy Rik Meeder)

This RABA 6x4 fire truck operated in RABA's home town of Gyor. (Courtesy Juraj Hlavac)

After its merger with Berliet, Saviem trucks were rebranded as Renault in 1978. (Courtesy Richard Stanier collection)

This Renault 6x4 sports the MAN-built 340bhp V8 diesel. (Courtesy F Michel)

Renault

In 1977, Berliet and Saviem merged to form the only HGV manufacturer in France – Renault Véhicules Industriels, the Truck division of the Renault Group. Saviem trucks were rebranded as Renault the following year, whilst Berliet continued building trucks under its own brand until the end of the decade.

ROMAN

Autocamioane ROMAN (with the DAC division) was a truck and bus manufacturer from Brasov, Romania. The company was established after World War II on the foundations of the old ROMLOC automotive factory built in 1921.

In 1967, as older Soviet-based trucks became old-fashioned, a tender was launched for a new diesel-powered truck range with a load capacity of 12-18 tons. As a result, Büssing, Mercedes-Benz, MAN, and UNIC offered technical know-how, but, in the end, a deal was struck with MAN.

This contract led to the construction, under licence, of two types of badge-engineered ROMAN trucks: a 135bhp medium-weight, and a 215bhp heavyweight. In the 1970s, DAC shared the same chassis cab with the ROMAN trucks, but it was not part of the 1971 joint-venture between the German company MAN and the Romanian government.

As the arrangement with MAN developed, ROMAN built bigger trucks, like this 19.256 6x4. (Courtesy Rik Meeder)

ROMAN trucks entered the UK in the early 1970s with licence-built MANs. (Courtesy Richard Stanier collection)

Saurer

Adolph Saurer AG was an Arbon, Switzerland-based manufacturer of trucks and buses, under the Saurer and Berna brands.

In 1959, Saurer launched its last truck design for highway use, the D-series, which was built in various configurations until the firm was taken over by Mercedes-Benz in 1982.

Saviem

Saviem was Renault's heavy truck division, formed in 1955 from the merger of Latil with the truck divisions of Renault and Somua.

The SM (Saviem-MAN) range had been introduced in France in 1967, with the 35-tonne SM 300 the most

powerful vehicle in the early Saviem range. It was built as part of a co-operation agreement between Saviem and MAN, whereby Saviem supplied cabs to MAN and, in turn, the German manufacturer supplied engines and axles to Saviem.

The SM 300 was powered by a naturally-aspirated, 15-litre V8 producing 305bhp, but it was not one of the newer engines developed by MAN in conjunction with Daimler-Benz. It was followed a year later by the SM32-240, which was initially launched in Europe, but arrived on the UK market later in the year.

The SM32-240 was supposedly designed for operation at 32 tonnes, but, with a puny 202bhp, it

The SM32-240 was supposedly designed for operation at 32 tonnes in the UK. (Courtesy Richard Stanier collection)

Saviem and Berliet were merged by parent Renault to form Renault RVI in 1977, and the following year Renault discontinued the Saviem brand. (Courtesy F Michel)

proved barely adequate for the UK's maximum permitted gross weight – trials were conducted by *Commercial Motor* magazine in March of that year. It was followed in 1975 by the SM280, fitted with a turbocharged MAN engine developing 285bhp SAE.

Scania

Following the establishment of the European Economic Community (EEC) in 1958, Scania-Vabis realised that it needed to set up a production facility within the Community in order to make inroads into the difficult French and German markets. So, having established an assembly facility in Zwolle in Holland in 1964, the Swedish manufacturer now had a bridgehead into five key European markets.

Around the same time, Scania also acquired Swedish cab builder Be-Ge Karosserifabrik, which had previously built cabs for both Scania and rival Volvo, and had already set up its own manufacturing facility in Meppel, Holland. Scania now had additional manufacturing space at Be-Ge's Swedish and Dutch plants, and set out on a major expansion programme.

Following the success of the LB76 trucks, Scania set even higher standards in truck design with the 1968 launch of the turbocharged 285bhp 110-series, which set a new bench mark for heavyweight trucks. However, not content to stop there, it went a stage further in 1969 with the launch of the thunderous 350bhp, 14-litre, V8-powered 140-series, which had the highest output of any off-the-shelf truck engine produced in Europe at the time – and this at a time when many British truck manufacturers were still fitting 150bhp Gardner diesels.

Scania's reputation for build quality, durability and power saw it enter the 1970s as the company to beat, and it certainly gave a lot of domestic British and European truck manufacturers a wake up call. However, not being a company to rest on its laurels it upgraded the 80-110-140-series in 1974 to the more powerful and even better equipped 81-111-141-series, with the 375bhp V8-powered top-of-the-range 141 shifting the goalposts even further.

Opposite top: Scania was one of the first European truck manufacturers to set up an assembly plant in South America. This colourful bonneted 111 is seen here in Argentina. (Courtesy Max Chern)

Opposite: The 111-series proved more than capable of handling heavy loads. (Courtesy Rik Meeder)

The Scania 141's V8 was upgraded to 375bhp in 1974, making it one of the highest output off-the-shelf trucks in Europe at the time. (Courtesy Lex Meeder)

Skoda

Skoda entered the 1970s with a range of trucks that had barely changed since their introduction in the late 1950s. The 706-series, produced in tandem with trucks bearing the Liaz badge, with its 150bhp, 11.8-litre diesel, had become left behind compared with the technical advances being made by truck manufacturers in Western Europe.

All Skodas were built with crew cabs – even the smallest four-wheelers. (Courtesy Juraj Hlavac)

Smoky, underpowered Skoda artics of the state-owned CSAD trucking outfit were a common site on European highways during the 1970s. (Courtesy Len Rogers)

Sisu

Having separated itself in 1968 from the state-owned Vanajan Autotehdas Oy, which manufactured buses and trucks under the Vanaja name, Sisu entered the 1970s with a range of 14 heavyweight trucks, in both normal and forward control options. The company had been using Leyland diesels from the late 1950s, but, by the 1970s, Rolls-Royce and Valmet diesels were also an option.

The forward control M-series was introduced in 1971, but, just three years later, Sisu returned to state ownership, and both the Rolls-Royce and Leyland diesels were phased out in favour of Cummins engines. Curiously, in 1976, Leyland and Saab-Scania each took a ten per cent stake in Sisu under a tripartite agreement. (Courtesy Rik Meeder)

Star

Fabryka Samochodów Ciężarowych, a Polish truck manufacturer based in the city of Starachowice, first started building 'Polish Star' trucks in 1948. It built rugged, if utilitarian trucks in various configurations.

Steyr

Steyr-Daimler-Puch was a large manufacturing conglomerate based in Steyr, Austria, with a reputation based mostly on military vehicles.

A bold move in 1968 saw Steyr launch its angular-cabbed forward control range of trucks and tractors, powered by its own 12-litre V8 diesel. (Courtesy Rik Meeder)

The Star 266 6x6 was introduced in 1973, with a 6.8-litre, 150kW diesel. It remained in production until 2000. (Courtesy Juraj Hlavac)

TAM progressed from its original Magirus-Deutz engine licence to a full mutual production plan with Magirus-Deutz in 1972. At its height, it employed more than 8000 workers. (Courtesy Juraj Hlavac)

TAM

TAM had quickly become Yugoslavia's leading truck manufacturer. In 1958, it began manufacturing vehicles under license from Magirus-Deutz in Germany, and, by 1961, the company was renamed Tovarna Avtomobilov in Motorjev Maribor (Maribor Automobile and Motorcycle Factory), though the TAM acronym and logo were retained.

Tatra

Tatra was a well-established vehicle manufacturer in Kopřivnice, Czech Republic, and, during World War II, was instrumental in the production of trucks, and tank engines for the German war effort.

In 1967, Tatra began production of one of its legendary off-road trucks, the T813, which used modular construction technology. It featured a new 19-litre, air-cooled, V12 diesel, which gave it a gross train weight capability of around 100 tonnes.

The Tatra T148 6x6 proved so versatile that there was hardly a job it couldn't tackle. (Courtesy Juraj Hlavac)

In 1969, Tatra decided to modernise its versatile 138 forward control range, resulting in the introduction of the 4x4 and 6x6 148-series, complete with a 12.6-litre, air-cooled V8 diesel, and a central spine tube chassis construction which allowed extraordinary levels of suspension travel, making it ideal for on-off road duties.

Did anybody actually want a 4x4 tractor unit? Tatra must have thought so as it produced a number of the T813 variants.

This Tatra T813 6x6 certainly makes an unusual recovery truck. (Courtesy Juraj Hlavac)

Terberg

Terberg built its first truck in 1966, using the running gear from an ex-army GMC 6x6 and the engine and cab from a Mercedes-Benz SF1200. With a huge demand in the late 1960s for on-off road construction vehicles in Holland, Terberg started modifying GMCs, and then switched to REOs and Diamond Ts as supplies of chassis ran out.

Terberg initially fitted both DAF and Mercedes components, and sourced a coachbuilt cab from Dutch coachbuilder Van Eck – the same cab as used by GINAF and early Scania-Vabis L75s.

Eventually, Terberg had to register as a truck builder in its own right and standardised on Volvo components.

Eventually, Terberg began acquiring cabs from local coachbuilder Van Eck. (Courtesy Rik Meeder)

Some of the first Terbergs were fitted with Mercedes-Benz cabs. (Courtesy Lex Meeder)

Once Terberg became a truck builder in its own right, it standardised use of Volvo components, including cabs. (Courtesy Rik Meeder)

UNIC

Originally a French car maker, UNIC started building trucks in the 1920s, and, by 1938, concentrated solely on the production of trucks.

Vanaja

Vanaja trucks were built in Finland by the state-owned Vanajan Autotehdas Oy, which manufactured trucks and buses under the brand name Vanaja until 1968, when Sisu took over activities at the Hämeenlinna plant. Some unusual Vanaja trucks were built, including those fitted with engines and cabs supplied by AEC.

In 1966 UNIC was taken over by Fiat, and eventually merged into IVECO in 1975. The brand did continue for a while on Fiat-engined Magirus trucks badged as UNIC. (Courtesy Rik Meeder)

Vanaja 8x4 crane truck fitted with AEC cab and AEC AV760 engine. (Courtesy Max Chern)

Volvo

Having gained a firm foothold in Europe in the late 1960s with its medium-weight F86 and super heavyweight F88 trucks, Volvo entered the 1970s as a pacesetter and was in expansive mood.

Following the launch of the 350bhp Scania 141, Volvo looked to develop more powerful engines with which to compete with its Swedish rival, and so developed the 330bhp, 12-litre engine, designed ultimately for a new series of trucks to be launched later in the decade. However, as something of a stop-gap measure, the engine was installed in an uprated F88 and called the F89. The F89 was an instant success and, as a result of some of the very first models being delivered to Russia, Volvo quickly became the leading supplier of trucks in the country.

In 1975, truck production in Belgium was relocated to a new factory alongside the car production plant in Ghent. Volvo had by now gained a firm foothold in Europe, and underwent considerable expansion there.

After many years leadership in the 28-ton plus category, Volvo finally came up with replacements for the long-serving F88-89 models at the Frankfurt Motor Show in September 1977 with the launch of the F10 and F12 models.

The Volvo F88 proved a pacesetter in heavy transport across Europe. (Courtesy Gyles Carpenter)

The Volvo F86 was a capable and popular medium-weight truck. (Courtesy Lex Meeder)

The excellent power-to-weight ratio of the F88 made it a popular choice with heavy haulage operators. (Courtesy Lex Meeder)

The G88 had a set-forward front axle for markets where this was a crucial requirement for hauling long trailers. (Courtesy Lex Meeder)

The F89 introduced Volvo's 12-litre, 330bhp diesel for the first time. (Courtesy Niels Jansen)

Volvo re-affirmed its leadership in the 28-tonnes plus category with the 1977 introduction of the F10 and F12. (Courtesy Rik Meeder)

Willeme

Founded in 1923 by Louis Willeme, the firm named after him had a short, but chequered life.

Early models were used by the French army and powered by an eclectic mixture of Willeme's own diesels, plus those from Deutz and AEC, and the company established itself as a maker of high-quality,   trucks. It even rebadged and sold both AEC and MBMC trucks in France.

Early Willeme trucks, such as this LD 201N tipper, were often powered by AEC diesels. (Courtesy F Michel)

Willeme established itself as a builder of high-quality trucks, such as this TL201HC, with an AEC AV 690 engine and 'Horizon' cab built by Cottard in Bourg en Bresse. (Courtesy F Michel)

Bankrupt by 1970, Willeme was taken over by Perez et Raymond, which continued to build Willeme's TG range of monstrous heavy haulage tractors with gross weights of up to 1000 tonnes. (Courtesy Lex Meeder)

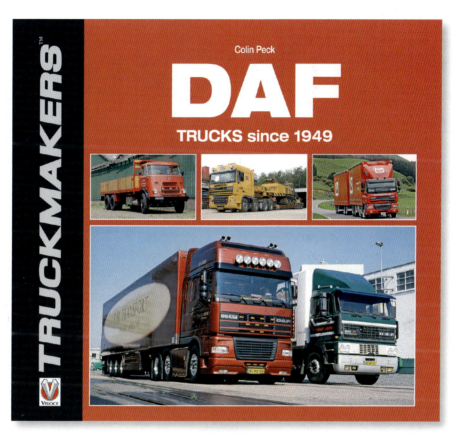

ISBN: 978-1-845842-60-4
Paperback • 19.5x21cm • £15.99* UK/$29.95*
USA • 128 pages • 120 colour & b&w picture
*prices subject to change, p&p extra

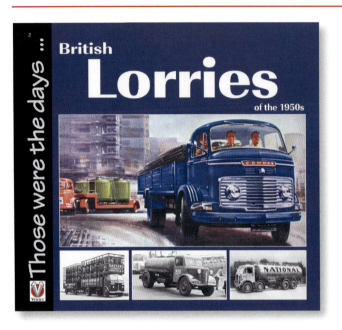
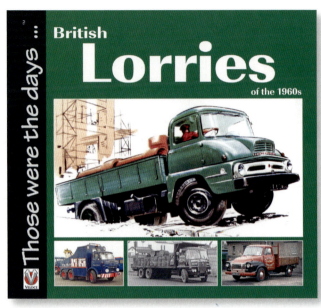

  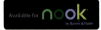   

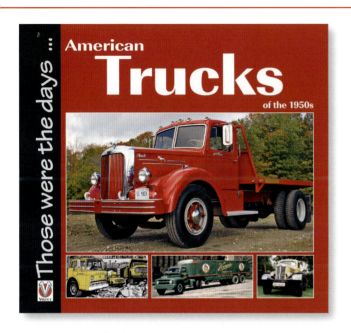

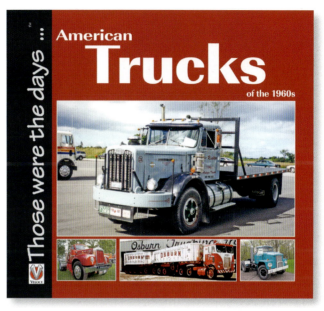

ISBN: 978-1-84584-227-7
Paperback • 19x20.5cm • £14.99* UK/$29.95* USA
• 96 pages • 124 colour & b&w pictures

ISBN: 978-1-84584-228-4
Paperback • 19x20.5cm • £14.99* UK/$29.95* USA
• 96 pages • 125 colour & b&w pictures

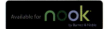

For more info on Veloce titles, visit our website at www.veloce.co.uk • email: info@veloce.co.uk • Tel: +44(0)1305 260068
* prices subject to change, p&p extra

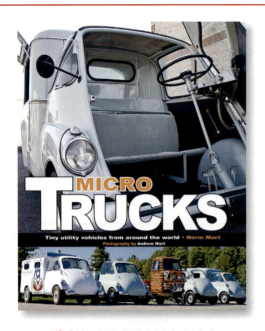

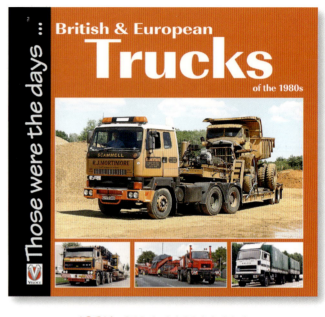

ISBN: 978-1-84584-175-1
Paperback • 25x20.7cm • ₤7.50* UK/$29.95*
USA • 96 pages • 100 colour pictures

ISBN: 978-1-845844-17-2
Paperback • 19x20.5cm • ₤14.99* UK/$29.95*
USA • 96 pages • 120 pictures

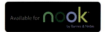

For more info on Veloce titles, visit our website at www.veloce.co.uk • email: info@veloce.co.uk
• Tel: +44(0)1305 260068
* prices subject to change, p&p extra

Index